The Monkey Pod Tree

By Mamoru Funai

Published by
American Buddhist Study Center Press
New York, NY

The Monkey Pod Tree
By Mamoru Funai

First Edition 2016

Copyright ©2016 by Mamoru Funai

Edited by Janet Revelt
Illustrations by Mamoru Funai
Designed by Brian Funai

Library of Congress Control Number: 2016957456

The Monkey Pod Tree
ISBN 978-0-9764594-1-5

Dedication

To Rev. Yoshiko Shimabukuro, for her inspiration and help
To Janet Revelt, for her tireless assistance and encouragement

To all who have helped with these stories:

Betsy Shimabukuro Oyakawa

Donald Ozawa

Mitsuye Kamada

Jean Funai Caswell

Barbara Funai Makizuru

Ellen Takeshita Asato

Brian Funai

Craig Funai

Hoshina Seki

Sara Barnett

Sue Manner

Francine Zephier

Christine Bajorek

The Artists' Circle

Sgt. Matsutada Makishi

100th Battalion/442nd Regimental Combat Team

All the people from Wahiawa, past and present

Table of Contents

Introduction

No one knows for sure, but the Monkey Pod tree in Wahiawa, Kauai, must be 100 years old by now. It grows in front of the Buddhist Temple, spreading its branches over the playground where children once laughed and played. Villagers consider that tree a landmark, and if it could talk, it surely would tell stories of life in Wahiawa. Of course, trees can't talk, yet some stories are meant to be shared.

The *Monkey Pod Tree* is a collection of stories told by a Japanese American boy, growing up in the small village of Wahiawa. The stories tell about the simple pleasures of the past, the meaning of family traditions, and the ties that bind friendships. Historical events change island life forever; however, the people of Wahiawa call on their courage to remain strong, while they continue to hope for a better life.

Wahiawa's New Arrivals

In 1898, during the early years of the McBryde Sugar Company, it became apparent that native Hawaiians did not like plantation work. As a result, Wahiawa (Camp 3) was established for the immigrant plantation laborers who were brought to Hawaii to work for the McBryde Plantation. In November and December of 1899, some of a group of 1,050 Japanese became Wahiawa's new arrivals.

From the beginning, most of these people planned to work as sugar plantation laborers just long enough to become wealthy. At that point, they hoped to return to Japan to live a comfortable life. However, the work was hard and the wages were small, and soon their dreams of returning to Japan faded. Eventually, with the establishment of a church and school, a sense of community developed and Wahiawa became their home.

The Great Bell

Every morning, Reverend Okawa, the head minister, dressed in his black robe and walked solemnly across the playground. He stopped under the great Monkey Pod tree, proceeded toward the stone steps leading to the Great Bell, and then paused. He clasped his hands, chanted a prayer, and pulled the rope that struck the Great Bell. The sound of the bell echoed throughout the village. The morning sun appeared in the sky, and in the distance, the old rooster crowed. This was the beginning of a new day.

Mother awoke to prepare breakfast of miso soup, rice, dried fish, pickled radish, and tea. As Father finished his breakfast, Mother made lunch for him. Then, Father climbed into the old sedan and drove to the company store. His job was to make deliveries to customers on the island.

Grandfather, or Gi-san as we called him, worked in the sugar cane fields. Like most men who came from Japan, he worked long hours under the hot sun, but received little pay. Most of the men dreamed of someday returning to Japan a little richer and, perhaps, to a better life. Gi-san sent most of his hard-earned savings to a Japanese bank in Kumamoto, because he, too, thought about returning to his family's home in Japan.

Before going home from the sugar cane fields, the workers went to a public bath house. Here, men and women had separate rooms in which to bathe.

3

At home, hot water was used only for cooking or for washing clothes. At the bath house, hot water for bathing was a luxury. After washing and rinsing themselves, the men and women climbed into a large hot water tub built with a partition down the middle. One side was for men; the other side was for women. They soon forgot about the many hardships, aches, and pains they had endured during the day.

Gi-san and Baba-san were in charge of the bath house. When Gi-san came home from the fields, he collected firewood from the valley. Every day Baba-san cleaned the bath house and filled the wooden tub with water, and then Gi-san built a fire beneath it. As the men and women came for their baths, they each put a few cents into a collection box.

While taking care of Fumi, Baba-san did laundry for the young Filipino men who had come to work in the sugar cane fields. They lived in another village several miles away. Every week, they brought their laundry to Baba-san to be washed. Their faces were dark brown from working in the sun all day, but they were always cheerful and friendly.

"Mamayan, I no come long time, bring many dirty clothes for wash," said Jose, speaking in Pidgin English, a dialect spoken by almost every Filipino worker.

"Das okay, Jose, I hab time wash today. I have ebe tin finis next week," said Baba-san with confidence.

Mother worked as a custodian at the elementary school in the town of Eleele.

"Don't forget to take your lunch, Michio," said Mother, as she and a neighbor left for work.

Michio met Pauly and Walto as they walked to their school in Eleele.

"Hey, wait for me." It was Teru.

"How come you're late?" Pauly asked.

"I had to do some stuff at home," said Teru. We all knew that Teru worked harder on his homework than we did, yet he didn't want to seem smarter than his friends. No one would be surprised if someday he would become a doctor or the president of a big company.

When school closed at 2:00 P.M., the boys walked along the railroad tracks, across the old wooden bridge, up the hill, and down the winding path that led them home. Sometimes, the boys stopped at a little store that sold all kinds of things, like bread, milk, canned goods, pencils, paper, sodas, and candies. In addition to food and supplies, the store had the only telephone in the village, which was used solely for emergencies.

"I found a dime on the way to the cafeteria today," said Alfie. "Let's stop at the store and get some candy." The boys got a bag of chewy candies and ate them on their way home.

"Baba-san, I'm home," Michio called to his grandmother, who was hanging the wash.

"Hello, Michio," Baba-san answered. "Are you getting ready to go to the Japanese school?"

"Yes," replied Michio. "I'll be home right after school."

The head minister rang the small bell that hung from the corner of the Buddhist Temple. It was time to start the Japanese Language School. The children assembled for the day's announcements. Reverend Okawa spoke clearly, "Children, next week we celebrate the Obon Festival. Therefore, classes will be canceled." The children were expressionless, but as they quietly went to class, smiles appeared on their faces.

"We can go biking to the beach," whispered Michio.

"Yeah, and then we can go swimming later," said Teru.

The lady teacher, or Sensei as she was called in Japanese, sat and waited patiently. She had a pleasant face, but seemed serious most of the time. In the classroom, the children sat and meditated for a few minutes. Some of the boys found it difficult to sit still even for a minute. It was tiring to attend the English School most of the day and the Japanese School later in the afternoon.

Sometimes, Sensei came quietly from behind and tapped a student's shoulder with a long stick. Sensei was strict, so she didn't hesitate to use the long stick on the back side of anyone napping. Today's lesson was learning to read and write Japanese from their textbook. Sensei paced the floor with the long stick held behind her.

On this day, Sho and Shun were playing basketball in the courtyard. They bounced the ball and tossed it through the hoop. Sensei looked out the window and said, "Please, stop playing this instant!" She spoke in Japanese, but the boys continued to bounce the basketball. Sensei left the classroom and confronted the boys in the courtyard. The children rushed to the window to see what was happening outside. Sensei spoke to the boys, and as she raised the long stick, Sho threw the basketball. It hit Sensei on the nose and knocked her down. Sho and Shun turned and ran as fast as they could. Later, after their parents found them, their fathers reprimanded them and punished them with a switch for bringing shame to their family names. Perhaps, this made Sho even more bitter and angry about being Japanese and being subject to strict traditional ways.

Sensei recovered, but she went about with a bandaged nose for several weeks. It was difficult for children not to stare at her. Somehow, she didn't look quite as dignified with a white bandage on her nose.

During the weekend, the older boys took Kendo lessons from the minister and teachers. They dressed in traditional Kendo uniforms and practiced the art of swordsmanship with bamboo swords, protective helmets, body coverings, and padded gloves. They bowed politely, and under the watchful eyes of Sensei, parried each other with their bamboo swords. They seemed to yell each time they thrust or made a move.

Michio and Teru sat alongside the Community Hall and watched as the boys practiced and Sensei looked on. "I would like to do Kendo someday, would you, Teru?" asked Michio.

"No, not me," said Teru. "You can get hurt banging each other on the head like that. I would rather ride my bike or go swimming!"

"Isn't that what the samurais do in the movies," asked Michio, "but with swords that look real? Hey, look. There's Takeo." The boys waved when Takeo looked their direction.

"Hi, guys, I'll see you later," said Takeo, as he went back to Kendo practice.

Baba-san was doing laundry for the Filipino men. It was hard work, but she never complained. She came from a rural village in Japan, and she kept her stoic ways of hard work and gratitude for another day. At times, Fumi helped Baba-san with the laundry. To entertain Fumi, Baba-san often sang children's songs from long ago. After the clothes were washed, Baba-san hung them on a line to dry. She felt the warm sun on her face, but working in the sun made her face brown and wrinkled.

"Baba-san, it's me," called Michio, "I'm in the mango tree. Would you like some ripe mangoes? I'll drop them into your apron, okay?" Michio climbed to the top of the tree where the best mangoes grew.

"You climb trees like a monkey," said Baba-san. "Be careful, Michio. Don't climb so high. It might get too windy up there."

"Don't worry! I'll be all right," replied Michio. "Spread out your apron, Baba-san. Are you ready? Here they come!" Michio carefully aimed and dropped the mangoes one by one. Baba-san caught each mango in her apron. "Good catch, Baba-san! Maybe you can be the catcher for our baseball team," said Michio.

Everything seemed to be going quite well until suddenly, a strong gust of wind swayed the tree and Michio lost his footing. Michio tried to grasp a branch, but it broke. He came crashing down to the ground. Baba-san rushed over to Michio. "Michio! Michio!" she cried.

Fumi began to cry when she saw Michio fall and lay still without moving. Baba-san looked up and prayed, "Oh, please, bring this child back to me." Baba-san shook Michio's shoulder. "Michio, wake up! Wake up!" She stood and called, "Gi-san, Gi-san, come and help me! Michio fell from the tree! Hurry, come and help me!"

Gi-san and Baba-san tried to revive Michio. His eyes fluttered and blinked, and he said weakly, "Baba-san, my arm hurts. I think it's broken!"

Baba-san clasped her hands and looked up to the sky. "Thank you! Thank you! It's only a broken arm."

Baba-san left Fumi with Gi-san and asked a neighbor to drive them to the doctor. The nurse helped Michio into Dr. Water's office.

"Well, young man, how can I help you today?" asked Dr. Water.

"Grandmother said that Michio fell from the mango tree and hurt his arm," said the nurse, "and that he's in much pain."

"Let's take a look at your arm," said Dr. Waters. "Looks like a clean fracture."

After the x-ray, the fractured arm was put into a plaster cast. "Come back and see me in a week," said Dr. Waters. "You were very brave, son. You did very well, but no more climbing trees for a while!"

It was dusk when Baba-san and Michio got home. Mother and Father had returned from work. The village men and women had finished working in the fields, had bathed at the bath house, and had returned to their homes for supper.

The evening sun slowly disappeared. The head minister was dressed in his black robe. He approached the Great Bell, chanted a prayer, and then rang the Great Bell. The resounding sound echoed throughout the little village. It was the end of another day.

Obon Festival

Obon is a Japanese Buddhist festival, usually held in mid-July or August. It is one of the most meaningful, enjoyable, and colorful of Japanese festivals. During this celebration, souls of dead ancestors are believed to visit. Prayers are said, especially for those who died in the previous year. According to beliefs, these souls need more guidance to bring them back from the spirit world. Vegetables and fruit are left out for the spirits to eat. Flowers decorate the graves or altars, and incense is burned.

During the week of Obon, bright red lanterns are hung everywhere. At one time, these lanterns were meant to guide spirits home from the spirit world. Now, the lanterns light the night for the festival dances and decorate the food and game booths.

Celebrations are held in the square, temple, or a vacant block of each town. A temporary wooden tower is erected in the center. At the top of the tower, a taiko drummer plays. Large speakers at the top of the tower play special Obon music, and men and women in "yukata," summer cotton kimonos, circle the tower and dance to the "bonodori." Bonodori are easy, rhythmic dances, said to calm the spirits of the dead during their visit. The dance is very simple and easy to learn.

Bonfires and fireworks are common. People frequently travel from town to town to see the different displays and dancing. Kyoto, a city in central Japan, is known for its display of burning rafts, which float on the river at the end of the week. These fiery rafts are believed to guide the ancestors back to the spirit world.

At the end of the week, bonfires and fireworks reach their peak, and the festival areas are taken down. Obon has ended for another year. Everyone returns home, and it is believed that the spirits return to their world as well.

The Festival

It was a warm, mid-July day in the little village of Wahiawa, located on the island of Kauai. "Wahiawa," an old Hawaiian word meaning "red soil," seemed the appropriate name for this little village, where sugar cane was grown in red soil for miles around. The villagers were happy, because this was the first day of the Obon Festival, a day to honor and celebrate the spirits of their ancestors.

Under the giant Monkey Pod tree, the village men were building food and game stands for the celebration. The younger men climbed the Monkey Pod tree and hung colorful Japanese lanterns from its branches. Michio climbed a ladder that was leaning against the tree.

"Hey, Takeo, I want to help, too," Michio called to Takeo.

"You're too young and small to be on the tree. You might fall and get hurt. This job is for bigger guys like us," said Takeo.

Takeo, Michio's next door neighbor, was well-liked and known for his quick smile. He had graduated from high school two years earlier. Everyone admired Takeo because he had been an excellent student and the best athlete in high school. He was a hero to the younger children, especially Michio. Someday, Michio wanted to be just like Takeo.

Within a few hours, bright red Japanese lanterns were strung on the Monkey Pod tree, and all was ready for the Obon Festival. Everyone gathered to observe a moment of silence while the minister conducted a welcome ceremony for the villagers, guests, and spirits, alike. The Obon festivities had officially begun!

The children immediately went to the game area. Fumi and her friends decided to play with a Fusendama, a colorful, thin, folded paper, which was blown up like a balloon. First, it was tossed into the air, and then it was volleyed back and forth. Michio and Teru watched.

"That looks like fun," Michio said to Fumi. "Let me try it!"

"Pass the Fusendama to me," said Teru.

"Hey, this game is only for girls," said Fumi.

"We don't mind. Let them play," said her friends.

So Michio and Teru played with the Fusendama ball.

After a while, Michio and Teru left the girls and walked to where the boys were playing Spin the Top. The object of this game was to try to knock the spinning tops out of a circle drawn on the ground. The boy with the last top spinning in the circle was the winner, and he was awarded a cash prize.

As evening approached, lanterns lit the school yard. On the wooden tower, an old phonograph machine played Japanese songs. The music sounded scratchy, but nobody seemed to mind. A big taiko, or drum, was fastened near the tower, where the drummer kept time with the music and danced to the beat. Dressed in their yukatas, Kiku, Mother, and Fumi joined with other ladies and danced around the tower. Soon, they were joined by other villagers, dressed in kimonos, Hawaiian shirts, or muumuus.

During intermission, the drummer on the tower beat the drum slowly. As more people came to dance around the tower, the drum beat became faster and faster. "Come on, Teru, let's join the crowd," Michio said. He and Teru had a wonderful time following the people as they danced around the tower.

"Look, Teru, there's Alfie," said Michio. "Come and join us, Alfie," Michio called out.

"Come join us," said Teru as he pulled Alfie by his arm. "Come on, Alfie!"

"You can do it," said Michio. "See, we just follow the leader!"

"Okay, but just for a little while," said Alfie. "I want to play Spin the Top before I play the last Bingo game."

Throughout the evening, more people came to the festival. Food stands sold hot dogs, teriyaki on sticks, cold noodles, shaved ice with strawberry topping, watermelons, homemade cookies, cakes, and sushi. The aroma of the teriyaki and hot dogs filled the air while the people waited patiently for their food orders.

The nearby Bingo stand was crowded. A man reached into a basket and called out numbers. Prizes were displayed behind him; the grand prize was a beautiful, red and white bicycle. It would go to the winner of the last Bingo game.

"Wow," exclaimed Michio. "That sure is a super bike!"

"I wish I could be the winner!" said Teru.

The Obon Festival continued late into the night, and people were slowly leaving. "Last Bingo game!" called the man into the speaker. "Here's your chance to win the grand prize, this beautiful bicycle!"

"I have two more tickets for the Bingo game. You can play one card, and I can play the other," Michio said to Teru.

"I have to go home soon," said Teru, "but I'll stay for this last game."

Just as the man called out the first number, Michio and Teru sat down at an empty game table. They waved to Alfie, who sat two tables away with several other boys. After a few minutes, Alfie shouted, "Bingo!" The man checked Alfie's Bingo card and called out, "We have a winner! You've won the bike!" Alfie had a big smile on his face.

"It's Alfie! He won the bike!" said Teru.

"What a lucky guy!" said Michio, "I'm so happy for him."

Earlier in the evening, a few men started a bonfire in the corner of the field. Now, everyone gathered to watch the flames, which were believed to guide the spirit world to the festival. Further down the field, fireworks brightened the evening sky.

"I had so much fun today, Teru. This is the best festival I've ever seen!" said Michio. I'm so happy it lasts for a week!"

"Me, too!" said Teru, "but now I have to go home."

Before leaving the festival, the boys stopped to gaze at the bonfire, and then, as they crossed the field, a fireworks display drew their attention.

"Wow, look at that!" exclaimed Michio.

"Look at that one!" added Teru.

No doubt, this was the perfect ending to the first day of this year's Obon Festival.

The Flood

It had been raining for several days. The river that flowed by the little town of Waimea began to rise, but no one was too concerned. The rain always stopped, and the river always went down.

Even on stormy days, school attendance was important. Students attending Waimea High School either took a bus or drove to school. Students attending elementary school rode in an old truck that had been converted into a school bus; others were driven to school by their parents. Many of the students, however, put on their raincoats and walked to school in their bare feet.

This particular morning, Kiku rode to the high school with her friends. Michio and Fumi started walking to school early in the morning. As they walked, Michio tried to hide his fear of storms from his sister. Whenever he saw a bolt of lightning followed by a crack of thunder, Michio shuddered and ducked his head. Lightning and thunder scared him the most.

"Come on, Fumi, hurry up," grumbled Michio. "We'll be late."

"I'm getting all wet," Fumi replied, trying to cover her head with a floppy rain hat. Michio held Fumi's hand as they ran toward the school. Mrs. Lyons, the teacher, helped them inside. "Hurry, children," Mrs. Lyons encouraged.

Mrs. Lyons was a tall woman with silver-gray hair and a ready smile. She wore wire framed glasses and spoke softly. "Come along, children, come along," she urged. Thunder and lightning lit the dark sky.

As the day went on, more rain fell, and a torrent of muddy river water covered the bridge that connected the highway to the town of Waimea. The river continued to rise, and soon, the little town's streets were flooded. Sirens wailed as the police and volunteer firemen evacuated villagers from their homes. Fishermen got their boats and rescued those who were stranded on rooftops of houses and buildings.

"Help, help, we're up here!" cried an old woman, holding her cat. "We'll be there. Just stay where you are!" said the fisherman. A call for more volunteers was sent out.

"We need all the help we can get," said the Mayor to the Police Chief. "Get the Army Reserves. Alert the hospital. This is an emergency!"

"Get all the people to the school grounds," shouted the Fire Chief. "Find more boats. Get anything that floats!"

The sporting goods store sent rubber rafts and surf boards. Soldiers stationed near the town came in Army trucks to help. Doctors and nurses came in ambulances to take people to the high school gym. Because electrical and telephone lines were out of service, it was almost impossible for parents to contact the school.

"Have you heard anything about Michio and Fumi?" Baba-san asked, her voice strained and anxious.

"No, not yet," said Mother," but I'm sure they'll be all right."

Eventually, word went out to most of the parents that their children were safe at the high school. For most adults, the day was worrisome. For many of the children, the day was adventurous. By evening, everyone would surely have a story to tell.

Jody, Alfie's sister, arrived home from the pineapple cannery just before the bridge was closed. She hurried to get her parents and Alfie out of their house.

"Hurry, get your belongings together! We have to leave before the flood water gets too high," she said. "Alfie, go and find Poi. We can't waste any time."

Alfie called for his dog, "Poi, Poi, come here, boy!"

"Over here!" Jody called to her parents. A fireman and a soldier were waiting in a boat by the window. Jody carefully helped her parents into the rescue boat.

"Come on Alfie, you're next."

"No, Poi isn't here!" cried Alfie.

As the fireman struggled to pull Alfie into the boat, Jody pushed him through the open window. Jody followed Alfie into the boat, and the boat started moving away from the house. At that moment, Poi jumped through the open window, missed the outstretched arms of the soldier, and fell into the water. The swift current pulled him down the river.

"Poi, Poi!" screamed Alfie, as he tried to jump overboard.

The men held Alfie back as Poi disappeared into the brown, turbulent water. Alfie broke loose from the fireman and jumped into the water. He tried to swim after Poi, but sank into the muddy water.

"Help him, please!" shouted Jody. "He can't swim!"

Before jumping into the water, the fireman tied one end of a rope around his waist and the other end to the boat. He found Alfie, pulled him up, and tied the rope around him. Alfie struggled and clung to the fireman. "Okay, now pull!" yelled the fireman. The soldier pulled the rope and finally got Alfie into the boat. It was a difficult, but successful rescue because Alfie was a big and heavy boy. Jody held Alfie close and rocked him gently as he wept.

Those who had been rescued were taken to the high school, where the military and Red Cross provided blankets and medical supplies. Volunteers from town served food and drinks. Jody and Alfie sat at a table with their parents, who were drinking hot tea.

"I wonder if the house is still there," said Jody's father.

"At least we are all safe," said Jody's mother.

Michio and Fumi walked by. "Hi, Alfie, where's Poi?" asked Michio.

"Poi fell into the water," said Jody, as she began to cry. Tears rolled down Alfie's face. Michio understood what had happened.

"They're serving hot chocolate. I'll get you some," said Michio.

"There are cookies, too," said Fumi.

"Okay," said Alfie.

When Michio and Fumi returned, they sat quietly with Alfie. The three of them drank hot chocolate and ate cookies together. This day was not a typical day.

Kiku, a student at the high school, had joined the kitchen volunteers serving meals to the rescued people. Takeo walked in.

"Hey, Kiku, how are you doing?" greeted Takeo.

"I'm doing fine," said Kiku. "It was very busy earlier,

but most of the people are fed now. How is it with you?"

"I'm helping to evacuate the folks still in town," replied Takeo. "I think everyone has been accounted for. I don't think we've had this kind of rain in a long time. OK, I've got to go. I'll see you later, Kiku."

The heavy rain stopped, but the flood water was still rushing rapidly toward the sea. The firemen and policemen moved their small boats along the flooded streets looking for anyone they had missed. They found a few cats stranded on the roofs of houses.

"Let's go back," said the fireman. "I think we've rescued everyone." As they turned the boat around, the fireman saw something on a rock near the mouth of the river.

"Look over there," he said. "Let me have your glasses."

"Let's get closer," said the policeman, and they moved closer to the rock. The sun was sinking toward the horizon.

Everyone at the school was very tired from the day's events. After Alfie fell asleep, Jody walked outside to see the flooded town below. Much to Jody's surprise, a rainbow began to appear in the distance. She

also noticed a fireman carrying a bundle in a blanket. He approached her and asked, "Are you missing a dog?"

"Poi, Poi, you're alive!" Jody exclaimed with joy. She took the little dog into her arms, and Poi licked her face. Jody carried Poi to Alfie and placed the dog beside him.

"Poi, you're back!' said Alfie, as he smiled sleepily and put his arms around Poi. Soon they both were fast asleep.

Jody put her arms around her mother and told her about the rainbow she had seen. "It's not such a bad day," said Jody. "We're safe and all together. I believe that the rainbow was a sign from the Hawaiian gods that all is well again!"

At the Beach

It was noon on a hot summer day. Michio walked under the Monkey Pod tree on his way to the basketball court, where Pauly, Walto, and Alfie were shooting baskets. Alfie, born with moderate Down's Syndrome, was bigger, taller, and older than the others, who considered him "one of the boys."

"Alfie, your turn to shoot," said Pauly as he tossed the basketball to Alfie.

Alfie bounced the ball on the back board. "I missed the basket," he said sadly. "I'm not good at this!"

"Keep trying," said Michio, as he walked onto the basketball court. "You can do it."

Alfie tossed the ball until it finally fell into the net. "Yeah, I did it! I did it!" Alfie said excitedly.

"I knew you could," answered Michio.

Alfie smiled, "Pass the ball to me again," he said.

After playing basketball for a while, Walto wiped his brow. "Boy, I'm sweaty. I could use a cold drink of soda."

"Hey guys, it's really hot today. Let's go to the beach," said Pauly. Just then, Teru rode up on his bicycle, got off, and picked up the basketball that had rolled away from the boys.

"Hey, Teru, we're going to the beach. Do you want to come along?" invited Pauly.

"Okay," said Teru, "that's a great idea!"

"Come on, everybody, we're all going swimming," called Walto.

"Let's go!" added Alfie and Michio, confirming the decision.

Michio imagined the cool, ocean water. He thought it would be a perfect day to practice his swimming and body surfing and to climb the coconut trees near the rocks. Going to the beach sounded like a great idea!

The boys began to walk down the red, dusty road to the beach. Along the way, they passed an occasional stone wall. Polynesians, the original inhabitants of the Hawaiian Islands, had built stone walls near their grass huts. The huts were long gone, but the stone walls remained.

Sugar cane grew along the side of the road. Walto and Pauly cut the cane with their pocket knives, peeled the stalks, and gave everyone a stick of sugar cane to chew. The winding road finally led to the beach, where coconut trees and a few sea grape bushes grew.

As the boys stood in the cool shade of the trees, they realized that walking to the ocean would be a challenge. The blazing, afternoon sun made the sand feel as if it were on fire. However, they decided that jumping into the cool water would be worth the pain of running on the burning sand. They all shrieked as they ran across the hot sand and dove into the water.

Pauly and Walto swam further out, where the waves were perfect for body surfing. Michio and Alfie swam near the shore and watched the older boys body surf. "Someday, I'll swim like the big guys," Michio said aloud. Just then, a big wave rolled in and washed Michio to shore. He wiped the water and sand off his face and then watched as Pauly and Walto rode another wave toward shore. Alfie was also caught in the big wave, and it tumbled him to shore. When Alfie stood up, his shorts were missing.

"Hey, look," yelled Pauly. "Alfie lost his shorts!"

"Here they are," called Walto. He threw them over Alfie's head, and another boy caught them.

"Hey, give them back!" yelled Alfie. Everyone laughed as Alfie ran around trying to catch his shorts. Alfie finally caught them, putting an end to the playful teasing.

Teru was sitting in the sand when Michio was washed ashore by the huge wave.

"You didn't get very far body surfing, Michio," said Teru.

"I was just practicing," said Michio. "Let's go by the rocks."

"Okay," answered Teru. He raced ahead of Michio, and then stood on the rocks, looking for the small fish that usually swam in the pocket ponds. "Look, Michio, the fish are in the pond," said Teru. "Ouch!" he cried out. "I stepped on a piece of broken glass!" He limped to the water to wash his foot. It was a small cut, but it bled steadily. Teru shut his eyes and moaned.

Michio examined Teru's foot. "Does it hurt? The cut isn't very big. You'll live," said Michio. "Stay where you are. I'm going to get us some coconuts."

Michio climbed the coconut tree like a monkey, remembering that Baba-san always said that he was a good tree climber. After all, he was born in the "Year of the Monkey!" Michio climbed to the coconuts and then hoisted himself to the very top of the tree. He sat there and gazed across the bluish-green ocean, enjoying its natural beauty. He saw whales in the water, spouting water-like fountains. The Island of Nihau was visible in the distance. "This is great," he said aloud, as the breeze swayed the coconut tree. "I feel like a big bird!"

"Hey, Michio, are you getting the coconuts?" called Teru.

"Oh, okay," said Michio. "Heads up, I'll drop them one at a time." Michio twisted a coconut off the tree branch and let it fall. After dropping

a few more coconuts, Michio began to carefully climb down the tree. He took one last look at the view, and at that very moment, he saw some-

thing moving in the ocean. A dorsal fin was heading toward the beach!

"Shark! It's a shark! There's another one! There are two of them!" Michio climbed down as fast as he could. "Sharks! Sharks! Get out of there!" he screamed to the boys in the water.

Teru turned and saw the sharks swimming toward shore.

"Sharks! Sharks!" he screamed. Teru forgot the cut on his foot and ran after Michio, who had started to run toward the water.

The sound of crashing waves muffled their warnings. Michio and Teru continued to scream. They jumped up and down and waved wildly, hoping someone would see them. Finally, Pauly and Walto spotted Michio and Teru, turned around, saw the shark's fin, and realized that the shark was heading toward them. The boys swam frantically until they reached the safety of the shore. Meanwhile, Alfie, who was in the shallow water, ran toward shore, not realizing that the shark was behind him. The shark opened its huge jaws, lunged forward, and snapped at Alfie's heels.

The big, gray shark rolled in with the waves. When the waves rolled out, the shark found itself stranded on the beach. It began to thrash about the sand. With the second round of waves, the shark flipped back into the water, was carried off shore, and began to swim in circles. While the boys stood on shore, they spotted the second shark swimming nearby. They continued to watch until the two sharks turned and headed toward the ocean depths.

"Did you see all the teeth in the shark's mouth?" asked Walto.

"That shark must have been at least eight feet long," said Pauly.

"This is the first time I've seen a shark so close," said Walto.

"Were you scared?" asked Michio.

"When I saw that big jaw with all those teeth, yes, I admit I was a little scared!" said Pauly.

"I was not going to let that shark take my shorts," Alfie said, "and he didn't!" Everyone laughed.

"I wonder how the sharks showed up so fast," said Walto.

"I've heard that sharks smell blood from miles away," said Michio. "Do you think they smelled the blood from Teru's foot?"

"Maybe they were after Teru's foot," Walto said with a chuckle.

"That cut is still bleeding," said Teru.

"That shark was hungry. See how far it got on the sand," said Pauly.

"That shark isn't the only hungry one," said Michio. "I think it must be suppertime, because I'm hungry, too!"

"Will you tell your mother and father about the sharks?" Pauly asked Michio. Walto, Teru and Alfie echoed the question.

"No," said Michio. "If they find out about the sharks, they'll never let me go to the beach again!"

"You're right!" said Walto.

"Okay then, no one say a word about the sharks!" advised Michio.

By this time, the clouds had already turned pink and red, and the sun was sinking slowly in the sky. It definitely was time to go home, so each of the boys picked up a coconut and began to walk down the winding road toward home. Going to the beach had been a great idea!

The Barefoot Football Team

The boys stood in line to be weighed for the Sugar Plantation Barefoot Football League, which was made up of teams from nearby towns and villages. Each team had most of its football equipment, except for shoes. Because football shoes were so expensive, it was ruled that all football players would play in their bare feet. The boys were fine with that rule; their feet were tough as leather from walking barefoot most of the time.

The games were played on Sunday afternoons at different fields. Almost everyone in the villages and towns went to the football games to cheer for their hometown teams. Some villagers walked to the games, while others came in trucks and cars. All arrived with box lunches and coolers of lemonade and cold tea. For Michio, it was like going to a festival or a carnival on a Sunday.

His neighbor and friend, Takeo, was on the football team. Takeo looked heavier than 135 pounds, the league weight limit, but he wasn't. He was, however, the best athlete from the village.

Michio was too young and too small to be on the team, but he was happy when the coach asked Alfie and him to be water boys. Each day after Japanese language classes, Michio met Alfie at the football field. As soon as they arrived, they filled the cooler with water, and then they watched the team practice. Both boys felt honored to be an important part of the team.

"I wish I were old enough to play football," said Michio.

"I'm old enough, but I'm too big and dumb," said Alfie.

"You're not dumb!" said Michio. "You can do many things that the other kids can't do. You're big and strong, and everybody likes you!"

Just then, Takeo called, "Hey, Michio, run for a pass." Michio jumped up and ran as Takeo threw the football. Michio reached for the football, but it slipped through his fingers.

"I should have caught that ball," mumbled Michio.

"That's OK," said Takeo. "You'll catch the next pass. It's practice time. I'll see you later." Takeo ran to join the other boys.

Sho and Shun stood watching from behind the baseball backstop.

"Michio, you're nothing but a big sissy!" taunted Sho, who was older and bigger than the other boys.

"Go and play with the girls!" yelled Shun.

"Ha, Ha, Ha," laughed Sho. "It's just as well they made you a water boy. You're good for nothing else!"

"Come on, Alfie, let's get the water to the football team," said Michio. As Michio and Alfie lifted the water cooler, Sho put his foot out and tripped Alfie. Alfie and the water cooler fell. Sho and Shun laughed and pointed fingers at Alfie. Michio helped Alfie to his feet. When Michio stood up, his fists were clenched. "Leave us alone!" he said, trying not to show the fear in his voice.

"You want to fight, do you?" Sho bullied, as he shoved Michio and then hit him in the face with his fist. As Michio fell backward, his nose began to bleed. The blow stung, and tears rolled down his face.

"Hey! Hey! What are you guys doing?" It was Takeo. "Cut it out!" Sho and Shun laughed loudly as they ran away. Takeo helped Michio to his feet. "Are you okay?" he asked. Michio tried hard not to cry, but the tears rolled down his dirty, bloody face. Takeo helped Michio wash his face,

and then he helped fill the water cooler. He walked with the boys to the football field. Michio was grateful that Takeo came when he did. Even though he cried in front of Alfie and Takeo, it was all right because they were his friends.

"Are you going to be OK?" asked Takeo. Michio nodded and said, "Yeah, I'm OK!" He and Alfie sat on the ground to watch the day's practice.

Early Sunday morning, Michio had cereal with bananas, half a papaya, and toast with pineapple jam for breakfast. He put on a blue T-shirt with "Wahiawa" printed on the front, and then jumped on his bike. Michio rode down the road to Alfie's house.

"Hey, Alfie, are you awake? It's time to go to the football field," called Michio.

"I'm almost ready," said Alfie, as he munched on a slice of banana bread. Alfie climbed on his new bike and rode down the road with Michio. The sun rose above the mountains, and soon it would spread its warmth on the villages below.

When Michio and Alfie arrived at the football field, they noticed that white chalk lines marked the field. That meant that everything was ready for the game. Michio and Alfie went to the locker shed where the football equipment was stored. Soon, the players would be there to "suit up" for the game. A few boys came early to run around the field, so they could lose a few pounds before weigh-in. If they weighed more than 135 pounds, they wouldn't be eligible to play in this season's first football game. Every boy definitely wanted to play in the first game!

As the morning went by, more and more people arrived at the field. The Lawai football team arrived in an old school bus. Their supporters followed in cars and trucks, waving their homemade banners and signs. It was as though a great battle was about to begin.

At noon, both teams lined up on the field and waited for the referee to signal the start of the game. The referee blew the whistle, and the crowd roared and waved their banners. The first football game of the season had begun. The Wahiawa team scored first, but the Lawai team scored soon afterwards. Encouraged by the crowd, the teams waged a see-saw battle.

"Come on, Takeo!" chanted Michio and Alfie.

"Come on! Come on, Takeo!" cheered Kiku, as she joined the boys. The older Issei cheered in Japanese, "Gambale! Gambale!" which means, "Fight hard! Fight hard!" It was the last quarter of the game, with Lawai leading Wahiawa 21 to 18.

The once clear blue sky had suddenly turned black. Thunder rumbled and lightning flashed in the sky. The Wahiawa team was 35 yards from a touchdown. "Field goal! Field goal!" everyone shouted.

Takeo was the only one who could kick a field goal, but he had hurt his foot earlier in the game, and the coach wondered if he could do it. With only seconds left, the team hurried into field goal position.

"How's your foot?" the coach asked Takeo.

"It hurts, but I'll kick," Takeo replied.

Takeo kicked the football high against the rain and wind. It landed and balanced on top of the goal post. Silence fell over the football field. Then, ever so slowly, the football flipped over for a field goal. "We're tied!" said the coach. "We'll get back and win this game!"

The referee called time out. "We have to call this game," he told the coaches. "This storm is too dangerous! The first Barefoot Football game of the season ends with a tie!"

Everyone ran to their cars and trucks for shelter. Michio and Alfie put the football equipment away.

"That was a good game, wasn't it?" asked Alfie.

"I didn't think Takeo's kick was going over the goal post," said Michio.

"Neither did I," agreed Alfie.

In the locker shed, Mrs. Kubo, the village midwife, dispensed first aid to the injured players. She examined Takeo's foot. "Looks as if you sprained your toe," she told Takeo. Then, Mrs. Kubo reached into her medical bag, found the tape, and bandaged Takeo's toe.

The football field was deserted when the boys left the locker shed. It began to rain harder, and by the time Michio and Alfie got home, they were soaked.

"I'll see you tomorrow, Alfie," said Michio.

Alfie waved goodbye, and said, "See you later."

Michio walked into the house, and when Mother saw him, she said, "Wash the mud off your feet, and get out of your wet clothes. Then sit down at the table because I have your dinner ready. Father and I have already eaten."

"Okay," said Michio.

"Michio, what happened to your nose?" asked Mother.

"Oh, nothing, I must have bumped it on something,"

31

answered Michio, not realizing that it had turned black and blue since his encounter with Sho earlier in the week.

Mother sat with Michio while he ate. She was eager to hear the details of his first day as water boy for Wahiawa's football team. She also hoped to hear the story of Michio's black and blue nose.

A Sunday Morning

It was a cool, quiet Sunday morning in the village of Wahiawa, on the island of Kauai, Hawaii. The sun was slowly rising above the mountains. Roosters were crowing to announce another new day.

Mother awoke first. She knocked on Kiku's bedroom door, and softly called, "Kiku, it's time to wake up." Next, Mother went into the kitchen to make coffee. As she began preparing breakfast, she turned on the radio to hear the news and the weather report. By this time, Kiku had washed her face and had come into the kitchen to help Mother prepare breakfast and set the table. Father climbed out of bed, wearing his yukata, a light summer kimono. Mother already had a cup of coffee ready for Father when he sat at the table.

"Breakfast," called Mother. "It's time to get up, Michio, and please wake your sister, Fumi!"

"It's Sunday. Why do we have to get up so early?" grumbled Michio.

"We're going to visit your cousins in Kekaha, and we don't want to be late," Mother replied.

"Oh, neat!" exclaimed Kiku. "Can I drive the car to Kekaha?"

"You have to speak to your father," said Mother.

"Father, can I drive the car to Kekaha?" asked Kiku.

"No," replied Father, as he sipped his coffee.

"But Father, I have a driver's permit and all I ..."

"No," Father replied firmly, "You cannot drive the car and that's that!"

Breakfast was being served when a voice on the radio announced, "This is a news bulletin. Pearl Harbor is under attack by Japanese planes." "Take cover! Do not stay out on the street! Take cover! Take cover!"

Mother and Father stopped eating and stared at the radio, trying to make sense of what they had heard. Michio's eyes widened, "Mother, Father, what is happening? Are we being attacked by Japan?"

Fumi walked into the kitchen and cried, "I'm scared! Mother, Father, I'm really scared!"

Kiku sat Fumi on her lap, put her arms around her, and said, "It's all right, Fumi. Mother, Father, Michio, and I are with you. Don't be afraid."

"Did you hear that? Did you hear?" It was Baba-san, who came quickly from the house next door. She, too, had heard the news on the Japanese radio program. "This is terrible! This is terrible! How can this be happening? It must be some kind of mistake!" Baba-san's voice quivered as she spoke.

Soon, news of the attack on Pearl Harbor was heard all over the world. Many ships and planes at the U.S. Naval Base were destroyed, and thousands of men and women were killed or wounded. Other military areas were also under attack and suffered many casualties.

Baba-san returned to her house. She and Gi-san knelt before their little altar to pray for those who died or were wounded. They prayed for the people and places that would surely suffer during the years of war.

Later, under a dim light bulb that hung from the ceiling, Gi-san and Baba-san sat on straw-matted floor cushions and talked. Gi-San said, "I've been thinking about my sister and her family living in Nagasaki, Japan. I wonder how they are doing with the news of the war with Japan."

"Yes," Baba-san sighed. "They have a grandson who is in the Japanese Navy. This is a sad time for everyone!"

"I fear very bad days and many hardships ahead for all who were born in Japan," replied Gi-san.

As Baba-san stared at an old photograph of Gi-san, she wiped tears from her eyes with her faded, old apron. That was the same picture he had sent to the matchmaker, or nakahodo, as he was called in Japan, who later arranged their marriage. When Gi-san left Japan for Hawaii to work as a laborer in the sugar cane fields, he was young and strong. Today, under the dim light, Gi-san looked old and tired.

Baba-san, who was 18 at that time, also sent her photograph to the nakahodo, who then arranged it so both families agreed to the marriage. The bride, who stayed in Japan, was married by a priest and officially registered with the groom's family. After the ceremony, Baba-san spent the next six months living like a servant in her mother-in-law's home. After the sixth month, Baba-san was permitted to join Gi-san.

To join her husband, Baba-san took a long boat trip from Japan to Hawaii. Other young ladies were on the same boat traveling to join their husbands. After the boat docked, Baba-san and the young ladies finally met their husbands. With photos in hand, Baba-san and Gi-san found each other. They both bowed and smiled. Baba-san thought Gi-san was handsome, but looked older than his picture.

Baba-san gazed at the photograph once more and wondered if she would ever see Japan again. Gi-san had fallen asleep on the floor, and as she gazed at his old, wrinkled face, whispered, "What a long time we have shared our lives together. How much more time will we have together in this world?"

In the weeks that followed, the village leader, the teachers, and the minister were questioned by the FBI. Non-Asian deputies searched every home for short wave radios and weapons. It was raining when men, armed with guns, identified themselves and walked into Michio's home.

"We're looking for short wave radios and guns," they said, as they looked through closets, dressers, and under each bed.

"We don't have any kind of weapons or radios," replied Father.

"I have a BB gun," said Michio, holding up his toy rifle.

"Don't bother us!" one of the men said gruffly.

"Look, Father, the men are walking around the house without taking off their dirty shoes," commented Michio.

"Keep quiet and go to your room," said Father.

After the men left, Mother and Father swept and mopped the floor. It was later reported that no short wave radios were found; however, the man who lived down the street owned a shot gun for hunting pheasants, and that gun was taken by the deputies.

A 7:00 P.M. curfew was enforced nightly, which meant that everyone had to be indoors by that time. Windows and doors of homes had to be covered with dark curtains or with black tar paper. The village committee assigned Father as Block Warden. He wore a white helmet with a BW painted on the front, and he carried a flashlight and a gas mask. It was his job to make sure everyone was in their home at night, with all windows and doors blackened out, and to alert everyone when there was an air raid.

During the weeks that followed, every family was instructed to make an air raid shelter near their home. Father and Gi-san decided the chicken yard would be the best place to build their air raid shelter. Everyone did their share of work until it was finally finished. Inside the shelter, there was a place to sit and a place to store food and water. The air raid shelter was braced with planks of railroad ties, which were then covered with sand bags and mounds of soil.

Gi-san didn't want all that soil covered with weeds, so he planted sweet potatoes. The potato plants grew fast, and in a few weeks, the air raid shelter was covered with sweet potato vines. Several months later, Gi-san handed a bucket to Baba-san. "Here's something we can have for supper," he said. Five sweet potatoes were inside the bucket. Baba-san made tempura sweet potatoes for a delicious supper surprise.

On February 19, 1942, President Franklin D. Roosevelt signed Executive Order 9066, which authorized the Secretary of War to declare certain areas along the West Coast as military zones. It also ordered the relocation of 120,000 Japanese Americans to different camps in the

United States. Of that number, just 38 percent were Japanese immigrants and resident aliens. The remaining 62 percent were Japanese American citizens of the United States.

There were 140,000 Japanese Americans living in Hawaii. Only those few who were considered security risks were sent to camps on the mainland. It was not uncommon for Japanese Americans (citizens of the United States) to return to Japan for their education. Upon returning to Hawaii, the Kibes (as they were called) were detained. Then, because of their ties with Japan, they were sent to holding camps in Oahu. There, they were questioned by the FBI, and those considered a security risk were sent to camps on the mainland.

At the same time, it was rumored that everyone of Japanese ancestry, regardless of where they were born, would be sent to one of the relocation camps in the United States. This caused worry for the people of Wahiawa, because they had never been to the United States. It also caused fear, because they dreaded leaving their possessions and homes.

Two months before the attack on Pearl Harbor, Reverend Okawa returned from visiting his parents in Hiroshima, Japan. It had been a long time since he had seen his parents. Upon his return to Wahiawa, he felt relieved that they were in good health. However, soon after the war broke out, Reverend Okawa was questioned by the FBI and ordered to leave for a relocation camp on the mainland. This news was a shock to the community and devastating to his family. Because this happened so suddenly, not many knew about his relocation order until the day two men in a black car drove into his driveway.

It was a cloudy day when the FBI escorted Reverend Okawa to the car. Only a few people from the village came to say good-bye. The ladies wept, and the men wished him a safe trip. Reverend Okawa turned to Mrs. Okawa and spoke briefly; then he turned to his children and held them close. "Teru, you are the oldest, so now you will be head of the family while I'm away," said Reverend Okawa. "Listen to your mother and look after your brother and sister. Don't worry. We will see each other again when this is all over."

Teru fought back the tears and said, "Yes, Father, I will do my best!" Reverend Okawa was helped into the car. Everyone waved good-bye.

Although all Buddhist ministers were sent to relocation camps on the mainland, Reverend Shima was an exception. She was born in Wahiawa and educated in Hawaii. Later, she studied in Japan, where she was ordained a Buddhist minister. Because Reverend Shima spoke fluent Japanese and English, she communicated well with the village people and officials. After the FBI interrogated and investigated Reverend Shima, they determined that she would be more useful if she remained on the island and served the people in Wahiawa and surrounding communities.

After Reverend Okawa was taken from Wahiawa, Reverend Shima's daily life became increasingly more difficult. The village people were Buddhists and needed a minister to conduct funeral services, marriages, counseling, and prayers for peace. Because her left arm was paralyzed at birth, driving a car would have been difficult, so she did not own a car. Neighbors or a family member often drove Reverend Shima to her appointments, and if no one was available, she took the bus.

One afternoon, Reverend Shima stopped to see Takeo's parents. "Hello, Mrs. Kishi. I was on my way home, and I thought I would pay you a visit."

"Oh, Reverend Shima, how good to see you," said Mrs. Kishi, "Please come in and have some tea with us."

"I wanted to check on you and Mr. Kishi and also to ask if you have heard from your son, Takeo."

"We are both well, and like everyone else, we are doing the best we can. We received a letter from Takeo, and he is fine, but he misses home and, of course, his friend, Kiku."

"My younger brother, Cho, also volunteered for the service. Quite possibly, Takeo and Cho are training together on the mainland," said Reverend Shima.

"Takeo said he is in Shelby, Mississippi. I have never heard of such a place," said Mrs. Kishi. "Is that somewhere in the United States?"

"Yes, it is one of the states in the South," replied Reverend Shima, "and very far from here. However, the boys from Hawaii will always take care of each other. Remember, traditionally, they wear the senninbari around their waist, to protect them from harm. Please, do not worry."

Mrs. Kishi recalled that she and the other women in the village sewed 1,000 red stitches on a white sash and gave it to Takeo before he left.

"I did not think I would be able to find enough people to sew all the traditional stitches on the senninbari," said Mrs. Kishi.

"Yes, my mother also made a senninbari for Cho," said Reverend Shima. "It took a while to finish it."

"I think of Takeo when I wake in the morning and when I go to bed at night," said Mrs. Kishi. "Can we send a prayer for the boys today?"

Reverend Shima and Mr. and Mrs. Kishi sat before the small shrine and prayed for the safe return of all sons and daughters. Reverend Shima looked at the clock on the wall. "I have another visit to make before I go home, so I'll have to leave to get the last bus for Eleele."

"Mr. Kishi can drive you to your next appointment, Reverend Shima," said Mrs. Kishi. "He has to stop at the post office in nearby Port Allen."

"Thank you, Mrs. Kishi; that would be most convenient, Sayonara." said Reverend Shima.

Mr. Kishi helped Reverend Shima into the old pickup truck and drove to Eleele. As she looked out from the truck, Reverend Shima noticed that several homes displayed a Service Banner. This banner was identified by its white field with a red border, with a blue star for each family member in active military duty. "Someday, I'll visit all the families displaying a service banner. I'll pray with them for the safe return of their sons and daughters," said Reverend Shima.

One day, several months later, when Michio came home from school, his mother called to him, "Michio, I have a letter for you from the mainland."

Michio washed his feet and wiped them on his pant legs as he ran into the house. A letter arriving from the mainland must be from Teru, he thought. He tore open the letter, and just as he had hoped, it was from Teru.

Dear Michio and all my friends in Wahiawa,

We were joined by many other people at the Honolulu harbor and then put on a big ship. This was the first time my brother, sister, and I were on such a big ship, so we were very excited. It took us about one week to sail to San Francisco, California. Haru was seasick for a few days during a bad storm.

In San Francisco, we were taken by ferry boat to a train. This was my first train ride. I always wanted to be a conductor on a big train, so I was very excited. As the train started up, it lurched forward. I tripped and fell and cut my chin. A retired doctor was on board. Mother gave him a needle and thread, and he sewed my chin.

The train took us to Arkansas, where we were put on buses that took us to an internment camp. We were all very tired when we got there, but fortunately, my family stayed together. We were assigned to an old Army barracks. A pot belly stove and Army cots are our only furniture.

Meals are served in a mess hall. Mother helps in the kitchen and the nursery, but she is not used to this type of work. I know she gets very tired!

We go to school every day, and everyone is in one classroom. Our teacher's name is Miss George. She is young and has a pretty smile. One day, it snowed and we were so excited. We made a snowman and even had a snowball fight! It gets very cold, so we wear many clothes,most of which are used. I even got to wear thermo underwear!

When the weather is warmer, we are allowed to go to the nearby woods, where we discover different kinds of animals, birds, frogs, and snakes. We use safety pins and strings on sticks as fishing poles. We find many things to do, but I miss swimming on the beach and eating mangoes and papayas with all of you. I hope we can come home soon.

We learned that Father was sent to a camp in Louisiana after he was taken from Hawaii. We are going to visit him in a few weeks. We miss him so much!

> *Your friend,*
> *Teru*

The rumor that all Japanese in Hawaii were going to be sent to relocation camps on the mainland did not take place, although the idea was seriously considered during the early part of the war. Logistically, it would be too costly to transport so many people to the mainland. Furthermore, the Japanese were essential to the economy and function of the Islands.

As the months went by, more and more men and women in the Armed Forces came from the United States. Michio had never seen so many Caucasians, or "Haoles," as they were called by his people. One day, when Michio was walking home from school, a young man approached him. "Hello, my name is Jim Cummins; I would like to speak to the leader of the village," he said.

Michio found Gi-san, who got Mr. Kishi, the interim leader of the village. The tall man introduced himself as a former Boy Scout leader,

now a sailor at the Port Allen Naval Station. He was very interested in forming a Boy Scout troop in the village. Mr. Kishi called a meeting for the Elders and parents. They decided that this would be a good time to have the boys learn about scouting and life in the United States. After the interview, they agreed that Mr. Cummins was a good man for the job.

When Michio heard about the Boy Scouts, he wanted very much to be in the troop. He hoped his parents would allow him to join the scouts. He was too young for the Boy Scouts, but just the right age for the Cub Scouts.

"Mother, I would like to join the Cub Scouts," said Michio. "I'll learn so many things, like how to build stuff, to camp, to learn first aid, to cook, and to take care of myself in the forest if I get lost."

"It will be all right with me," said Mother, "but Father must give the final approval." At supper that night, Michio asked Father about joining the Cub Scouts.

"No, you may not join the Cub Scouts," said Father sternly.

"Let him join the Cub Scouts," said Baba-san. "He will need something to keep him busy during the vacation months."

"We have saved some money, and it can be used to buy his uniform," said Gi-san, as he lit his pipe.

Michio was happy to be a Cub Scout. Perhaps, someday, he would be a Boy Scout, but for now, he was happy in his blue Cub Scout uniform. Mr. Cummins was a kind and gentle Scout Master. At times, he invited his friends to teach the boys carpentry, gardening, and first aid. One Sunday morning, Mr. Cummins assembled the boys and drove them to the Christian church in the town of Eleele. This was the first time most of the boys had stepped foot inside a Christian church. Unlike the Buddhist Temple, they didn't have to leave their shoes at the door.

During the service, a lady played the organ, and a choir sang hymns. The Haole minister, Reverend Blane, spoke most of the time. Michio and some of the other boys began nodding their heads, and Michio soon fell sound asleep.

After the church service, the boys were invited to the meeting room for cookies and punch. The boys thought this was the best part of going to church. Everyone greeted them with a friendly smile. "Hello boys," said Reverend Blane, "Welcome to St. Andrews Church!"

Reverend Blane had white hair, a kind face, and a large red nose that made him look a little like Santa Claus. He went around shaking everyone's hand. The pretty, gray-haired lady had a beautiful smile. She hugged each of the boys, and when it was Michio's turn, he closed his eyes and tried to pull away. In spite of acting silly, Michio liked it very much. He couldn't remember when anyone had ever hugged him.

Whenever Mr. Cummins had a day off, he took the boys on hikes, showed them how to cook, and taught them first aid. Afterwards, when evening came, they all climbed up the hill to look at the clear, starry sky. "See there. That's the Little Dipper; over there is the Big Dipper; there's the North Star," he said to the boys as he pointed to the sky. "See there to the right. That's Leo the Lion." Michio thought Mr. Cummins was the smartest man in the world. He wished his father were a little more like Mr. Cummins.

One day, when the boys and Mr. Cummins were on the school playground, an Army jeep stopped in front of the Buddhist Temple. Two soldiers got out, walked up the steps, and went into the temple.

"Excuse me sir, but this is a Buddhist Temple, and it is proper to leave your shoes at the door before entering," said Mr. Cummins.

"Who do you think you're talking to?" snarled the driver.

"Get out of here!" ordered the other soldier.

The soldiers walked around the temple, looked behind the drapes and walls, and wrote on a clipboard. Names of those who had died since they had come to work in the sugar cane fields were written in the back cupboard. The following day, dozens of trucks roared into the courtyard, and soldiers in full battle gear jumped out. Most of the soldiers were young men, like Takeo.

It wasn't long before favorite places looked so differently. The Japanese School was occupied by the U.S. Army. The beach, once used for picnics, fishing, and swimming was lined with barbed wires. Machine guns were camouflaged along the hillsides.

Months went by, and everyone tried to help with the war effort. Families, encouraged by the government's suggestion to grow their own fruit and vegetables, planted gardens. These gardens, called "Victory Gardens," gave everyone a feeling of patriotism. Adults bought U.S. war bonds and saving stamps. The Scouts went into neighborhoods to collect aluminum pots and pans. Michio proudly wore his uniform when they marched in the Fourth of July parade.

One day, a military car drove to the Kishi home. An Army officer got out and knocked on the door. As soon as she opened the door, Mrs. Kishi knew why the officer was there. She clutched the telegram and collapsed to the floor. Her neighbors, who had been watching from their homes, rushed to Mrs. Kishi's side. They also knew what was to come when they saw the Army officer.

Takeo had been killed in the Vosges Mountains in France, along with many others in his platoon. It happened in October, when the weather was getting colder and rainy. The 442nd had the difficult job of rescuing the 141st Regiment, a foot battalion, which had been surrounded by enemy soldiers.

It was a warm, sunny day when the funeral service for Takeo was held at the Kishi home. Reverend Shima conducted the service, and everyone from the village and the island came. Kiku stood with her arm around Mrs. Kishi's shoulder. As they held Takeo's last letters close to their hearts, they both wept.

Mr. Cummins and the Scouts, dressed in their uniforms, stood outside with most of the Kishi's neighbors. One of the boys played taps as Mr. Cummins and the Scouts stood at attention and saluted. Michio felt very proud to have been Takeo's good friend. As he thought about Takeo, the tears welled in his eyes and rolled down his cheeks.

Once, Michio imagined Takeo with the football and calling to him, "Run for the pass, Michio." When he turned around, it was Alfie, not Takeo, standing behind him.

"Hi Alfie," greeted Michio.

"Are you going to watch football practice tomorrow?" Alfie asked.

"I suppose so," answered Michio, "but it won't be the same without our friend, Takeo."

Other young men from the 442nd Battalion were killed during the war. Homes displaying Service Banners with a gold star, edged in blue, now represented a family member that died during military service. Reverend Shima conducted a funeral service for each of these families.

It was the summer of 1945. The cities of Hiroshima and Nagasaki were devastated by the Atom Bomb, and the news of Japan's surrender was heard over the radios. Sirens wailed and whistles shrilled throughout the towns and villages.

"Baba-san, Baba-san, the war is over! We defeated Japan!" exclaimed Michio. "Now everyone will come home again!" Baba-san knelt before the

little Buddhist shrine in the corner of the room and prayed for her family and the country she would never see again.

Reverend Shima climbed the steps to the Great Bell, clasped her hands in prayer, and rang the bell. The sound echoed throughout the village. People stopped whatever they were doing, turned their heads toward the Bell, and bowed their heads in prayer. The war had ended, but many would not be coming home to cool, quiet mornings, to the sun rising above the mountains, and to roosters crowing. The villagers knew, however, that those beginnings of a new day would once again bring hope for a better tomorrow.

Teru's Trip to the United States

Reverend Okawa left Wahiawa in February of 1942. In December of 1942, Mrs. Okawa received an official letter from the authorities ordering the family to relocate to a camp on the mainland. At the end of the year, they would go to Honolulu for a few days and then go to the United States. Perhaps they would be able to reunite with Reverend Okawa.

"Teru, be sure to bring only a few of your belongings. We won't be able to take many things on this trip. Please help Haru and Kimi with their bags," said Mother. When they were ready to leave, they waited at the end of the driveway. An old car drove up. "Hello, Mrs. Okawa and children. I'm here to drive you to the boat at Na willi willi," announced Mr. Kishi.

"I made some lunch for you to take on your trip," said Mrs. Kishi.

Another woman approached Mother and said, "Mrs. Okawa, I'm Reverend Shima. I came to pray for you and to wish you a safe journey."

Many people from the village came to say goodbye. The ladies all wept and cried. The men bowed and said a few words of encouragement to Mrs. Okawa and the children. Teru's sister, Kimi, held onto her mother and cried.

As he rode his bike toward his friend, Michio called out, "Teru, where are you going?"

"To a boat at Na willi willi; then to a place in Honolulu for a few days; then to the mainland, and maybe we'll meet my dad," replied Teru.

"Maybe we can go swimming when you get back home," said Michio.

"Or maybe we can shoot baskets," said Teru, as he wiped a tear from his eye. The boys said their goodbyes, and Teru got into the car. He sat in the front seat with Mr. Kishi. Haru, Kimi, and Mother sat in the back seat.

Teru waved to his friends as the old car traveled down the bumpy road toward Port Na willi willi. Clouds rolled in from behind the mountains, and it began to rain softly. Kimi began to whimper and pressed closer to her mother. "I'm cold and I'm scared," she whispered.

"It's going to be all right," Mother reassured her.

"We'll all miss you and your family," said Mr. Kishi. "Have you heard from your father, Teru?"

"Yes, we have," answered Teru. "I think he and some of the other ministers are in a camp in Louisiana."

"A letter from him arrived not too long ago," said Mrs. Okawa. "He is fine and hopes that he'll be able to see us when we get to the mainland."

Teru recalled what his father had said to him on that fateful day. "You are the oldest, Teru, so you are now head of the family. Listen to your mother and take care of your brother and sister."

Teru felt sad as he looked out the window and watched as the cane fields, little houses, and shops disappeared from sight. He wondered whether he and his family would ever return to his Hawaiian home. He promised himself that someday he would return.

At Port Na willi willi, many Japanese Americans waited to board the small boat that would take them to Honolulu. Each person carried one small suitcase. Mother spoke with some of the other families. As they huddled under their umbrellas, everyone looked worried and bewildered.

In Honolulu, they were taken by bus to the relocation center. After a few days at the center, they were taken to the Honolulu water front pier, where the people waited to board a big gray passenger liner.

"What a great ship! I hope I'll have a room with a window so I can see the ocean," said Teru.

Haru looked worried. "I just hope I don't get seasick!" he said.

Soon after everyone had boarded the ship, a young girl passed out song sheets. A young man encouraged the passengers to join him in singing Christmas carols. It was Christmas Eve, December 24, 1942, and singing made things a bit more cheerful. It didn't matter that most of the people were Buddhists.

Later that night, under a starry sky, the gray passenger ship sailed out to sea. "It will take about a week to reach San Francisco, California. That's plenty of time to see the ship," said Teru to Haru.

"A week is a long time," said Haru. "I hope I can last that long. I don't feel good! Goodnight, Teru, I'll see you tomorrow morning."

The next morning, Teru awoke early to a bright, sunny day. He joined Haru on deck, where they stretched out on deck chairs and watched sea gulls flying above. "Look over there! Dolphins are following us," said a man, who was leaning against the rail. Teru hurried to the rail and saw three dolphins swimming with the ship.

"Come here, Haru! Look at the dolphins! They're trying to race this passenger ship!"

Haru leaned on the rail. "Oh, Teru, I don't feel good! I'm going back to sit on the deck chairs."

Teru was excited to sail on this big ship. He watched people play shuffleboard and toss horseshoes. He pretended that he was on a vacation cruise, but later that night in bed, Teru thought about his family's journey. Would father meet them on the mainland? Would the family stay together? Where would they live?

It stormed most of the following day. The ship tossed and rolled in the waves, so everyone stayed in their rooms. Haru remained in bed all day. Being seasick was not fun!

After a week, the ship reached the port of San Francisco. Over 1,000 Japanese Americans were transported to shore by ferry boat. First, they were examined by doctors and nurses. Next, they were questioned and processed by officials. Then, they were assigned to different camps around the country. Last of all, the families were put onto buses and driven to the railroad station.

This was the first time that Teru was on a train, and he was very excited. "All aboard!" called a man in a blue uniform, "All aboard!" The train traveled through many little towns. The window shades were pulled down, and the passengers were not permitted to look outside. When the train stopped, people on the platform shouted and jeered.

Sometimes, children threw stones at the moving train. The travelers did not understand these strange events.

Teru was afraid, but he wanted to be brave in front of his family. "Don't worry. Everything will be all right," he said. Just as he finished speaking, the train lurched forward and Teru tripped and cut his chin. Mother tried to stop the bleeding with a towel.

"I can't stop the bleeding. We need a doctor!" she said anxiously. "There's a doctor in the next car. I'll bring him to you," said the conductor.

"What do we have here?" asked the doctor when he saw Teru. He examined Teru's chin, and then said, "I'll have to close that cut. Mother, do you have a needle and thread handy?"

Mother found her sewing box and gave it to the doctor. Because the doctor didn't have medication for Teru, he put a small towel into Teru's mouth. Then, he began to sew the wound. Teru shut his eyes tightly and bit down on the towel. Tears rolled down his cheeks, as he muffled the screams that welled up from his throat. The doctor bandaged Teru's chin and said, "Teru, you have been an excellent patient!"

"Thank you very much," said Mother. "Where is your hospital? I would like to pay you."

"No," said the doctor, "There's no charge for this service. I'm retired, and my patients are usually animals. I'm a veterinarian."

Finally, the train stopped in Arkansas, where the detainees boarded Army trucks and were taken to their new homes. The families soon learned that "home" would be one of many barracks which had been occupied by soldiers. Each barrack was empty, except for a pot belly stove and several Army cots.

"Teru, we'll need firewood. See if you and Haru can find

some outside," said Mother. The boys asked a neighbor where they could find some firewood. They were directed to a shed, but when they opened the door to the shed, it was empty.

"What do we do now?" asked Haru.

"We'll look along the fence," replied Teru. "There must be firewood somewhere!" The boys walked along the barbed wire fence.

"Hey, you boys, get away from there!" a guard shouted gruffly from the tower. A shot rang out, and it hit the top of a tree.

Teru and Haru ran as fast as they could. As they ran, Haru tripped over some lumber. They quickly picked up as much wood as they could and carried it to their new home. That night, Mother and the children pulled their cots close to the pot belly stove. It had been a long day, and everyone was very tired. It wasn't long before they were fast asleep.

In the morning, Teru and Haru shivered as they walked to the outdoor toilet. Teru couldn't imagine that anywhere could be as cold as Arkansas.

"I need a warm breakfast," said Haru, his teeth chattering.

"Me, too!" said Teru. "Let's hurry. We're to meet Mother and Kimi at the Mess Hall."

The Mess Hall was in the center of the compound, surrounded by rows of Army barracks. Teru and Haru met Mother and Kimi, and then they joined the long line of people waiting to have breakfast. They sat at a huge picnic table to eat their breakfast of cold cereal, toast, and powdered eggs. This food took away Teru's hunger, but it would never be as good as his mother's breakfast meals at home!

A boy about Teru's age sat next to him at the picnic table. Teru spoke first. "Hi, my name is Teru. What is your name?"

"My name is Eddy," answered the boy.

"I'm from Hawaii," said Teru, "where the weather is always warm."

"I'm from California, and the weather is warm there, too," replied Eddy.

"I don't like this cold Arkansas weather!"

After breakfast, Mother took Haru and Kimi back to their barracks. While the children quietly played together, Mother wrote a brief letter to Reverend Shima....

Dear Reverend Shima,

In spite of the adjustments that had to be made, the children and I are fine. We haven't heard from Reverend Okawa, but I assume he is well. He has always been dedicated to his health and taking care of himself. We miss him and hope we will be able to meet with him soon.

I was concerned about the children and how they would adjust to the change of seasons, but somehow they have adapted well to their surroundings. I count the days until we return to Wahiawa and be with you again.

Until we meet again,
Mrs. Okawa

Because school-aged children were expected to attend class, Teru and Eddy walked to the school building together. They sat next to each other in the classroom and became instant friends. A hush fell upon the room when the teacher entered.

The teacher was young and had a pretty smile. "Good morning, boys and girls. My name is Miss George," she said, as she wrote her name on the board. "Let's begin the day by saying the Pledge of Allegiance to the Flag of the United States." The students stood, placed their right hands over their hearts, and recited the pledge.

The day's lesson reviewed very much what Teru and Eddy learned at their schools in Hawaii and California. Later in the afternoon, when the boys looked out the small classroom window, they saw snowflakes drifting from the sky.

"Eddy, I've never seen snow, is that snow?" whispered Teru.

"That is snow; it's really snowing!" Eddy whispered excitedly.

The boys patiently waited for class to be dismissed for the day. As they walked home from school, Teru and Eddy saw Haru and Kimi running to meet them. They, too, were excited to see snow for the first time. They jumped around and tried to catch the snow with their tongues. They hoped it would snow until the ground was totally covered.

"If we get more snow, we'll be able to build a snowman," said Haru.

"Yeah," said Eddy. "We can build a fort and have a snow ball fight! If only we had warmer clothes."

That afternoon, a truckload of firewood was delivered to the camp. That evening, a second truck delivered boxes of used clothes and shoes, which were distributed among the people. "Look, everybody," said Teru, "my first pair of thermo underwear! I never thought I'd ever have to wear so many clothes at one time to stay warm!"

It snowed almost every day for several weeks. On the weekend, after all the chores were finished, the boys met at the basketball court.

"Let's build a fort," said Eddy.

"We'll build a snowman, too," said Teru.

"I want to help build the snowman," called Kimi, as she ran toward the boys.

"We better make a pile of snowballs," said Haru. "I have a feeling we need to be ready for a snowball fight!" The boys worked a long time, and finally, the fort was completed. With Kimi's help, they built a snowman nearby, and Eddy stuck a small American flag in the snowman's hand.

"This is for my big brother in the Army," said Eddy.

"I didn't know you have a big brother," said Teru.

"Yes, Kenny is in the Army, and he's stationed somewhere in France," Eddy said proudly.

Suddenly, a snowball smashed into their fort.

"Watch out!" said Haru, "We're being attacked."

"Kimi, I hear Mother calling you," Teru yelled. "It's time for you to go inside." Teru watched as Kimi ran to Mother, and then he turned toward Eddy and Haru and shouted, "Get the snowballs ready! Here they come!"

It didn't take long for Teru, Eddy, and Haru to become winners of the camp's first snowball fight. They were sure to be challenged again, but they wouldn't mind. Playing in the snow was fun.

Suddenly, a feeling of sadness came over Teru. Until now, his fun had always included Michio and Alfie. Teru missed his friends in Wahiawa, and he decided that it was time to write them about his trip to the United States.

As Spring followed Winter, days became routine, but memories of home were always present in the hearts of Mother and the children. It was especially exciting when a letter arrived from Wahiawa. Mother eagerly opened the letter and began to read...

Dear Mrs. Okawa,

I was very happy to hear from you. I'm glad to hear that you and the children are adjusting to camp life. It must be difficult to get used to the change of seasons, especially during the winter months.

Because I am the only available minister here, there are many services to arrange. Most of my work have been the funerals for the Issei, who, as you know, are the first generations who came to Hawaii from Japan. Also, there have been a few funeral services for the young men who were killed in Italy and France. It saddens me greatly to do this, for I have known them since they were little children in school.

Please do take care of yourself and your children. You remain in my prayers.

> *Sincerely yours,*
> *Reverend Shima*

Mochi-tsuki

Mochi is a special food treat served for Oshogatsu, the Japanese New Year. It is a sticky rice dumpling, with a soft dough-like texture. It can be eaten plain, with different sauces, sweet stuffing, or seaweed.

When mochi is used as a spiritual offering, it represents hope for a happy and bright year ahead. For this, two mochi cakes are placed on a sheet of pure white paper in the center of a wooden tray. Then, the tray is placed near an altar.

To make these treats, sweet rice is washed and soaked overnight. In the morning, the rice is steamed. Next, it is put into an usu (a large stone bowl) and pounded with a kine (a wooden mallet). After the rice becomes soft and smooth, it is put on a floured table, where it is shaped into soft, chewy cakes.

At one time, mochi-tsuki, or mochi pounding, was an important part of Japanese New Year festivities. This day-long tradition brought family and friends together, telling stories, singing, and happily ending the old year and beginning a new year. Times change, however, and now, it is not uncommon for people to purchase mochi from a store. Regardless, mochi remains part of the Japanese New Year tradition.

The New Year

It's almost the New Year," said Baba-son. "Michio, come help me with the stone bowl." The bowl, called the usu, was chiseled from a big stone and was used to make the traditional mochi for the New Year celebration. As Grandmother cooked the special sweet rice used to make the mochi, Michio washed the large stone bowl.

After the rice was cooked, it was placed into the usu. Men using wooden mallets, called kines, kneaded the cooked rice until it was soft and sticky. Only then was it ready to be pounded into dough.

Baba-san dipped her hand into a pan of water before she turned the rice over. Next, the men rhythmically pounded the rice until the mochi was smooth and sticky. The mochi was then put onto a floured table. The ladies completed the tradition by shaping the rice into individual, round, flat cakes.

"Omedeto, Omedeto! Happy New Year!" said the neighbors when they came to take turns making the mochi. Soon Baba-son's little house was filled with people. The men drank sake and began to sing songs from long ago. Baba-son played the shamusen, a three-stringed instrument she had played when she was young. Today, she was that young girl again, playing the shamusen as everyone sang. Many wept, for they felt that this could be the last time they would celebrate the New Year together.

Mother recalled the day Takeo told her and Father that he wanted to volunteer for military duty. His father objected when he learned of Takeo's plan. "Takeo, I disapprove of you volunteering. Think of what this will do to your Mother! She will get sick from worrying about you," Father said firmly.

"Let him go," pleaded Mother, "This is something he must do. This is our duty if we are to stay here, to let him go. This is our country now." She wiped the tears from her eyes. "Go Takeo, and join your friends."

"Don't worry so, Mother. I'm going to be all right. All my friends are volunteering, and we'll take care of each other," said Takeo.

Mother remembered how Takeo had jumped on his bicycle and hurried down to the recruiting center. Later, Takeo told her that it seemed as if all the young men who graduated with him had the same plan, including Cho Shima, the Reverend's younger brother.

"Hello, everybody!" called Reverend Shima. "I stopped to see how everyone is doing this New Year."

"What a pleasant surprise, Reverend Shima! Happy New Year! Come in, come in," said Baba-san. "Many of the neighbors are here today. Please say a prayer for the young men going into military service soon."

"Of course I will," replied Reverend Shima. "I would be most honored."

Baba-san placed a mochi cake on a dish before the statue of Buddha, and then lit a candle. Everyone sat on the floor as the minister conducted the prayer service. She prayed for the mothers and fathers, and she prayed for world peace. Some of the mothers wept softly.

After a few minutes of silence, Gi-san said, "Let's celebrate the New Year and hope for the best!" He began to sing, and the others joined in.

"Hi, everybody," Takeo called out. "I came to help with the mochi-tsuki!" He got the kine and said, "It's my turn to pound the mochi."

Just then, Kiku came. "Hello, everyone, Omedeto Gozaimasu, Happy New Year!" She put on her apron and sat down with the ladies at the table. Takeo and Kiku had been friends since elementary school. Everyone knew that someday they would marry and raise a family in Wahiawa.

The mochi making lasted all day, and almost everyone who came to help brought food and drinks. Michio was enjoying the teriyaki and mochi soup, his favorite foods.

"Can I pound the mochi, too?" asked Michio.

"You're too small to lift the mallet," said Takeo. "Try again next year."

"I am not too small!" said Michio firmly. "See, I'm strong enough to lift the mallet." Michio raised the wooden mallet above his head and fell backwards.

The men laughed. "Come back when you're bigger and stronger!" they said.

The aroma of steamed rice and charcoal-grilled teriyaki chicken filled the air and added to the festive mood. The men pounded and chanted in unison, stopping only when Baba-son turned the mochi. The ladies chatted about their children, grandchildren, and their new sushi recipes. The men recalled the big fish they caught along the shore in Kekaha. Some had relatives in Japan and wondered about them. Joy seemed to be in the air, but beneath it all loomed the reality that their sons would soon go off to war.

By early evening, the last batch of mochi had been made and wrapped. Mochi-tsuki had been very special, but the curfew had to be observed in the little village, as it was throughout the island. Baba-san wished "Omedeto" to all and gave each family some mochi to take home.

Kiku took a cup of green tea and sat outside under a mango tree. The tea tasted good, and it helped her to relax. She gazed at the clear sky and marveled at the bright stars. Takeo came outside to join her.

"What are you doing out here, Kiku?" asked Takeo.

"I'm just looking at the stars while I'm enjoying my tea," Kiku replied. "The stars seem so far away and so beautiful!"

"I believe all the stars came out tonight just for us," said Takeo.

"Takeo, when are you leaving for Oahu?" asked Kiku.

"Next week, Tuesday," answered Takeo. "We leave at 11:00 A.M. from the airport."

"I'll miss you very much," said Kiku.

"I'll miss you and everyone here in Wahiawa," replied Takeo.

Kiku tried very hard to hold back her tears. "You'll take care of yourself, won't you?" she asked.

Takeo reached out and held Kiku's hand. "I'll be okay. Don't worry. I'll be back before you know it. There's a whole group of us leaving together, and we'll look out for each other."

"I'll write to you every day," Kiku promised.

"And I'll write to you whenever I can," said Takeo. Both knew that this particular Mochi-tsuki would always hold a special meaning for them.

The happiness of Mochi-tsuki faded within a few days. Tuesday morning, the sun shone brightly in the deep blue sky, and the morning air smelled pleasantly fresh. Neither hinted that this would be a sad day for so many in Wahiawa.

It was a short ride to the airport. Takeo drove the old car. His father sat beside him, and the rest of the family sat in the back seat. Mother held a lei on her lap; its fragrance filled the silent car. There wasn't much to say.

The airport lobby was crowded. Many families and friends had come to send their young men off to Oahu, where they would join other inductees. Takeo looked for Kiku, but then he remembered that this was a school day, and Kiku would still be in class.

"Attention everyone, we're taking pictures of the inductees. Please stand in front of the airplane," said the photographer. The men stood in line, each wearing his best Hawaiian shirt. At least one flower lei was around each young man's neck. Some of them had so many leis that their faces were hidden. Just then, a girl ran toward the inductees.

"Takeo, Takeo, I made this lei for you," Kiku said as she put the lei around Takeo's neck. "Goodbye, take care of yourself!"

Takeo put his arms around Kiku. They held each other, and this time the tears fell freely. Takeo wanted to say something, but he couldn't think of anything to say, except, "I'll miss you, Kiku. I'll miss you."

A loud voice announced, "It's time to board the airplane!" The young men said their last goodbyes, and then they walked through the gate. The airport lobby became unusually quiet, as family and friends waved good-bye. No one left until the airplane was just a speck in the deep blue sky.

Takeo's Journey

Takeo was one of 2,685 Japanese American Volunteers assembled on the grounds of the Iolani Palace in Honolulu. The palace was built in 1882, originally as the residence of Hawaiian Kings and Queens. Formerly, it was the seat of the Territorial Government, but now, it was headquarters for the Military Government.

As the volunteers gathered, well-wishers arrived to see the young men go off to the mainland to be trained as soldiers. Thousands of people joined their loved ones for the farewell ceremony, perhaps for the last time. There were speeches by officials and dignitaries and music by the United States Army. There were flower leis and hula girls, a Hawaiian Aloha tradition.

Although he didn't expect to see anyone he knew, Takeo looked over the crowd. It would have been an expensive trip for his parents to see him in Honolulu, yet he was certain he heard his name called.

"Takeo! Takeo!" It was Kiku, holding Mrs. Kishi by her arm. They waved and came towards him.

"How did you get here?" asked Takeo, putting his arms around his mother and Kiku.

"Friends and neighbors donated money for our trip," said Kiku, as she handed Takeo an envelope. "They also wanted you to have this cash envelope. Buy something for yourself when you get to the mainland."

"Father wanted to see you, too, but instead, he asked Kiku to come in his place," explained Mother. "We're happy to be here, but for now, we're taking you to lunch at a Japanese restaurant."

"It's so great to see you," Takeo said warmly. "I can't believe that you're really here!"

A few days later, the Japanese American Volunteers boarded the S.S. Lurline and set sail for Oakland, California. After a week, the ship reached port, and the men continued by train to Shelby, Mississippi, for training. Here, they joined the 100th Battalion, comprised mostly of Japanese Americans from the Hawaiian National Guard, which had arrived in Shelby two months earlier from combat training at Camp McCoy in Wisconsin. The men of the 100th Battalion chose to patterned themselves after the (Issei) first generation Japanese way of their parents. This created a positive impression of Japanese Americans with the military and with the people of Shelby, Mississippi.

The Japanese Americans from Hawaii, however, had their own unique life style. Unlike the Japanese American (Nisei) second generation counterpart from the mainland, they patterned themselves after the Polynesians of Hawaii. The Hawaiians spoke rapid Pidgin (a mixture of English, Chinese, Filipino, Japanese, and Hawaiian). They wore bold, brightly-colored Hawaiian shirts, sang Hawaiian songs, played ukuleles, and wore zories or went barefoot. Because they were accustomed to walking barefoot on the islands, wearing Army boots was the biggest problem for the Hawaiians. They were extremely loyal to one another. If there was a fight against one Hawaiian (Buddhahead), it became a fight against all Hawaiians. The word "Buddhahead" did not hold a religious meaning; instead, it was a play on words, as "buta" means "pig" in Japanese.

Because the mainland Japanese Americans kept to themselves and spoke stateside English, the Hawaiians believed they were trying to be like the mainland Caucasians. They also thought they were cheap because they spent their money carefully. Many harsh words and frequent fights exploded between the two groups. The Hawaiians called the mainlanders Kotonks, because the sound of the mainlanders falling during a fight reminded the Hawaiians of the sound of a coconut falling and splitting open.

Many times, Takeo tried to stop his Hawaiian friends from fighting, but it was useless. One night, Takeo rescued a Kotonk from a fight by pulling him out through a door.

"Are you okay?" asked Takeo.

"Yes, I'm okay, just a bloody nose and a few lumps," the young man replied. "Thanks for getting me out of there. Why did you help me? You know I'm a Kotonk."

"Not everyone looks at things the same way," answered Takeo, "and I'll do my fighting with someone else. By the way, my name is Takeo. What is yours?"

"Mine is Kenny."

Takeo continued, "Where is your hometown?"

"San Mateo, California," replied Kenny. "How about you; where's your home, Takeo?"

"I'm from a small village called Wahiawa, on the island of Kauai," answered Takeo.

"I'm not even going to try to pronounce that name," said Kenny. "That's Hawaiian, isn't it?"

"Yes, it is Hawaiian. I think it means red dirt, but no one knows for sure," answered Takeo. "Where is your family now?"

"They are in a relocation camp in Arkansas," said Kenny sadly. "We had a vegetable farm in San Mateo once. We had to sell the farm when we were ordered to relocate to a camp in Arkansas."

"Some people were sent to relocation camps from the Islands, but not like all of the people from the West Coast," said Takeo. "I'm sorry you and your family were sent to the camps. It must have been tough to volunteer for service after all that," Takeo said in an understanding tone of voice.

"It's getting late, Takeo, and I'm a little sore, so I'll be heading back to camp. Thank you for helping me," said Kenny.

The company commander became aware of the conflict between the Buddhaheads and the Kotonks. One day, he decided to take a group of 10 Buddhaheads with passes to visit Rohwer Relocation Camp, not far from Camp Shelby. The Hawaiians thought they were going to a party, so they were in a good mood. They sang songs and played their ukuleles as they rode along in the truck.

When they got to Rohwer Relocation Camp, they found the camp enclosed by barbed wire fences. They were invited to dine with the people, who offered them the small amount of food they had saved. The Hawaiians were humbled by this act of kindness, but they declined the invitation to stay for dinner. Their ride back to Camp Shelby was somber.

"I wonder what I would have done if my family were put into one of those camps," began Joe. "Would I have volunteered so eagerly?"

"Now I understand why the Kotonks are so frugal," continued Masa. "They send their pay checks to their parents in the camps."

"I'm going to donate a little of my pay to the people at Rohwer each month," announced Joe.

"Same here," added Masa, and soon everyone repeated, "Same here!"

Word got around to the other Buddhaheads about the visit to Rohwer Relocation Camp, and soon after, tension began to ease between the Hawaiian Buddhaheads and the mainland Kotonks. Takeo was pleased that the two groups finally came to an understanding.

Before the war began, 14,000 Japanese Americans were serving in the Hawaiian National Guard. In addition, Japanese Americans from the mainland were in different military units throughout the United States. These groups of soldiers eventually combined to form the 100th Battalion, the first segregated Japanese American unit in the United States Army.

After several ideas for their color, an identifying badge, pennant, or flag, the 100th Battalion made their final choice. Their colors showed a helmet that was worn by ancient Hawaiian Chiefs and the ape leaf to ward off evil spirits. They also chose a Battalion motto, "Remember Pearl Harbor."

The men were trained in Hawaii, with additional training at Camp McCoy, and finally at Camp Shelby. From there, they were sent to Oran, North Africa. They departed for Italy to join the 34th Division of the 5th Army. In combat, the 100th Battalion fought gallantly, like true heroes. The Japanese American soldiers were focused on one important idea. They would proudly prove their loyalty and duty for their country, the United States of America.

After a year of intense training, the 442nd Regiment earned their colors, which was a hand holding the torch of liberty. Their motto was "Go for Broke," Hawaiian slang for "shoot the works." They were now ready to join the 100th Battalion in Italy.

Months later, when the 442nd Regiment landed in Italy, the 100th Battalion had already established themselves in combat. They won praise and respect from their commanding generals and from the local people they liberated. The men of the 442nd Regiment hoped to earn the same respect.

Takeo awoke earlier than usual. He was uneasy about the day's assignment and calmed himself by writing to Kiku...

Dear Kiku,

Today the sun came out, and it was great to feel its warmth. Funny, I never paid much attention to the sun when I was on the Islands. Today, if nothing else, I've learned to appreciate things that we take for granted.

Some day when I get home, I'll lay on the beach with you beside me until the sun sets into the horizon and wait for the stars to appear in the clear, dark sky.

I remember the time we went fishing for Biobio and Michio came along. He wanted to know the names of the constellations. Has he learned all the names of the stars?

Yesterday, Kenny joined our company as a medic. He must have gone into medical training soon after basic training. It was great to see him again.

If we make it through today, I hope the sun will be out again tomorrow. Take care of yourself and all my love to the family and friends.

Aloha, with love,
Takeo

"Hey, Kenny, how do you feel now that we're where the real fighting is going on?" asked Takeo, as the two men climbed into the Army truck on the way to the front line.

"I don't know. There's a lump in my stomach," said Kenny. "I think I'm just scared!"

"Yeah, me too!" said Takeo.

Just then a soldier waved and called out, "Hey, Takeo, it's me, Cho, Cho Shima. Remember me? We played football together at Wahiawa!"

"Sure, I remember," answered Takeo. "You're Reverend Shima's younger brother. How are you doing, Cho?"

"I'm okay. I'm just going back to get supplies. Maybe I'll see you later." Cho's truck rumbled down the bumpy, muddy road. The boom of artillery and the rattling of the machine guns could be heard in the distance. Takeo hoped he could be tough enough to get through this.

Months passed and the 100th Battalion and the 442nd Regiment fought bravely in the battle of Belvedere, Italy. They were awarded the Distinguished Unit Citation and the 100th and the 442nd were officially combined into one unit. Later, they were sent to southern France, where they encountered and fought more battles with German troops.

Takeo tried very hard to keep his promise to write Kiku as often as he could. "Free" time was rare; however, Kiku and Wahiawa were always in his thoughts. Takeo's letter began...

Dear Kiku,

October in France is cold and damp and is the preview of what is to come in the next few months. I never thought too much about the change of seasons, but now I'm very much aware of the weather and watch the ever-changing skies. Most of the guys from the warmer climates are getting use to the cold weather. I wear several pair of socks, but my feet still feel cold at night.

Yesterday was Sergeant Kubo's birthday. The Sarge was in the Army before the war started, and he looks after us like a "mother hen." Hiroshi, our cook from Maui, made rice and a pot of sukiyaki. Of course, Hank played his uke and got everybody to sing "Happy Birthday." Later, we all sang a few of the old Hawaiian favorites. Can you believe that most of us forgot the words to the songs! Most importantly, Sergeant Kubo enjoyed his birthday. It was a good time for everyone.

We'll be leaving early tomorrow morning for somewhere. Until next time, take care and Aloha to the family and friends.

Aloha, with love,
Takeo

Later, during a lull in the fighting, the men rested along the streets of Bruyeres, France. Takeo reread two letters from Kiku...

Dear Takeo,

It was so good to hear from you. After school, I always stop at the Post Office to check whether a letter has come from you, and today it did! I'm happy to hear you are safe and well. I'm happy to hear you met Kenny. He seems like a good friend.

It must be difficult for him to think about his family in the "camp" and try to perform his duty as a medic. Perhaps, we can send letters to cheer him and to let him know how much we appreciate him taking care of you and the men in your company.

Mother and I often visit your mom and dad. They are keeping themselves busy working in their garden. They had a good season for tomatoes, cucumbers, and radishes, so the vegetables were given to the neighbors.

Reverend Shima came to visit one day, and we prayed for your safe return. She keeps in touch with Mrs. Okawa and her children, who as you know, are in a Relocation Camp in Arkansas. It must be difficult to start all over again so far away from home.

Michio writes to Teru whenever he can. Teru, Haru, and Kimi were excited to see snow for the first time. Teru's friend, Eddy, has an older brother named Kenny, who is in the 442nd Regiment in France. Could it be that your friend Kenny is Eddy's brother?

In spite of objections from Father, I finally got my driver's license. I'm driving to the hospital and helping as an aide. I'm thinking of going to nursing school.

I'll write again soon. Take care of yourself. We all miss you.

> *Aloha, with love,*
> *Kiku*

Dear Takeo,

Everyone is doing fine here, and we are trying our best to help with the war effort. I am attending nursing classes at the hospital, so we'll be prepared in an emergency. One day, perhaps, I will study to be a nurse and work in a hospital.

Your mother and father are busy working in the garden most of the time. This year, they had a good crop of cucumbers and radishes. They are making pickles out of the cucumbers.

How is the weather where you are this time of year? Did you get used to the change of weather there? I heard it can get very cold and snowy during the winter months. Your mother and I knitted a pair of woolen gloves and a scarf for you to wear.

We also baked some macadamia cookies and mochi candies for you to share with your friends.

Your mother said to be sure to wear the senninbari all the time. We all miss you very much and hope you will come home soon.

Aloha, with love,
Kiku

Takeo read Kiku's letters over and over. He held them close to his face and took a deep breath. He felt as though she was there with him. His thoughts were of the many things that had happened since the war began and how this war would change lives forever.

"Letters from home?" asked Kenny.

"Yeah, it's good to hear from them, especially from a girl from my hometown," replied Takeo. "How about you, Kenny, got any news from home?"

"I get letters from my mother and sometimes from my kid brother, Eddy. They seem to be doing okay and doing the best they can, living as they are," Kenny said sadly.

"I've got to hand it to you and the others who volunteered to be in this. It took courage to join up!" said Takeo.

"I heard from the grape vine that we're moving out to rescue the "Lost Battalion" of the 141st Regiment with the 36th (Texas) Division. They got cut off from the rest of their regiment," said Kenny. "I also heard this isn't going to be a family picnic!"

For a while, Takeo gazed at the mist that covered the Vosges Forrest. His mind wondered to thoughts of Wahiawa and to those he loved. He sat down, and wrote a letter to Kiku...

Dear Kiku,

Here I am a world traveler. First, I saw the States, then Italy, and now I'm in France. Who would have imagined that a guy like me from Wahiawa would be seeing all these places!

I have met many good people along the way. Some are from Oahu, Maui, Kauai, the United States, and, of course, the people in Italy and France. The people in Europe have suffered many hardships, and they are grateful we have come to help restore peace to their homeland.

Someday, when this war is over, perhaps you and I can take a trip together, and I can show you where I have been and the people I have met.

Thank you for all the nice things you have sent me. I'm looking forward to the macadamia cookies that you have made. Thank you for looking after my mother and father.

Take care of yourself. I miss you very much.

Aloha, with all my love,
Takeo

"OK you Buddaheads and Kotonks, get on your feet! We're moving out at 0200," yelled Sergeant Kubo. "We're going to rescue the "Lost Battalion" of the 141st Regiment!"

"Hey, Sarge," said Takeo. "If by chance I don't make it back, would you make sure my letters get to my family?"

"Yeah, sure," said Sergeant Kubo, "but we're all making it back, and we're all going home, so don't even worry about it!"

Sgt. Kubo tried to boost the men's moral, but he knew what was foremost in their minds. It was even difficult for him not to think what might happen. A few days earlier, the 1st Battalion of the 141st Regiment with the 36th Division was separated from the rest of the company. Several rescue attempts were made by the other battalions, but they were driven back by the Germans.

Days later, on a cold and rainy October day, the men of the 442nd Regiment and the 100th Battalion made their way through the rugged hills and valleys of the Vosges Forrest to rescue the 275 men of the "Lost Battalion." They encountered the Germans, who were trenched in along the hills and ridges. After days of fierce fighting, the 442nd Regiment and the 100th Battalion finally broke through the enemy resistance and rescued the "Lost Battalion." Although the rescue was successful, the 442nd and the 100th suffered many casualties.

It was a sad day when Sgt. Kubo collected the ID tags, called dog tags, of the men killed in action. Then, he kept the last promise he had made to his men. He sent letters home to their families.

Epilogue

After World War II ended, the villagers of Wahiawa regained hope for a better tomorrow, but that hope came with many changes. Gi-san, Baba-san, and their Issei friends and neighbors lived the rest of their lives in Kauai. They never returned to Japan. Father and Mother moved to a small house in Lihue. Michio and his friends continued their education. They went to high school; some went to college in Hawaii or on the Mainland. The sugar cane plantations and the pineapple industry closed. Small villages like Wahiawa became empty and still. The Buddhist Temple in Hanapepe, Kauai, eventually became the home of the Great Bell. In time, the Japanese School, the Community Hall, and the Buddhist Temple existed only as memories, as did all the activities they hosted.

Some years later, while visiting his parents, Michio drove his father's car up the winding road to Wahiawa and parked the car. Everything he remembered was gone, everything except the old Monkey Pod tree, which stood as strong and tall as he remembered. With its branches reaching out over the silent playground, it seemed to be protecting every memory of Wahiawa for those who returned.

Bibliography

Asahina, Robert. Just Americans: *How Japanese Americans Won a War at Home and Abroad.* New York: Penguin Group, 2006.

Hazuma, Dorothy Ochiai and Jane Okamoto Komeiji. *The Japanese in Hawai'i.* Rev. ed. Honolulu: Bess Press, 2008.

Okubo, Mine. *Citizen 13360.* Seattle: University of Washington Press, 1983.

Yenne, Bill. Rising Sons: *The Japanese American GIs Who Fought for the United States in World War II.* New York: St. Martins Press, 2007.